ISBN 978-0-260-55348-5
PIBN 10955792

Historic, Archive Document

Do not assume content reflects current scientific knowledge, policies, or practices.

U. S. Department of Agriculture
Washington 25, D. C.

OFFICIAL BUSINESS

BAE-DPS-2/51- §500
Permit No. 1001

Penalty for private use to avoid
payment of postage $300

BUREAU OF AGRICULTURAL ECONOMICS
UNITED STATES DEPARTMENT OF AGRICULTURE

WASHINGTON, D C   ᛒᕼᕮ   FEBRUARY 1951

Approved by the Outlook and Situation Board March 5, 1951

CONTENTS

	Page		Page
Summary	1	Fats, Oils and Oilseeds	13
Output and Employment	3	Corn and Other Feed	14
Income and Related Factors	5	Wheat	15
Commodity Prices	6	Fruit	16
Agricultural Exports	8	Commercial Truck Crops	17
Farm Income	10	Potatoes and Sweetpotatoes	18
Livestock and Meat	10	Cotton	18
Dairy Products	11	Wool	19
Poultry and Eggs	12	Tobacco	20

SUMMARY

Economic activity in the Nation continues to expand. Although production for defense is increasing rapidly, output for civilian use remains at a high level. Demands for most goods and services have intensified, reflecting expanding incomes to consumers and business, and prospects for some reduction in civilian supplies, primarily of durable goods, later in the year. The consumer buying wave during January and February was similar to the sharp rise which occurred last summer following the outbreak of the Korean conflict. Business, also, has sharply increased inventory holdings. Food supplies available to civilians this year are likely to be somewhat larger, on a per capita basis, than in 1950.

The general level of wholesale prices has been fairly stable since mid-February at a level 1.6 percent above that immediately preceding the effective date of the General Ceiling Price Regulation and 16.2 percent above the pre-Korean level. Wholesale prices of farm products and of foods declined in the last week of the month while a slight increase occurred for industrial products.

The persistent downtrend in the value of agricultural exports in most of the post World War II period continued through most of 1950. However, a sharp increase in value of exports occurred in the last quarter of the year, 27 percent above the third quarter and only slightly below the comparable quarter in 1949. For the calendar year 1950 as a whole, the value of agricultural exports totaled 2.9 billion dollars, one-fifth less than in 1949 and more than a fourth below the record year of 1947. The physical volume of agricultural exports declined 17 percent from 1949 to 1950 primarily due to a sharp drop in exports of wheat and flour.

Item	base period	Year	Jan.	Oct.	Nov.	Dec.	Jan.
Industrial production 1/							
Total	1935-39=100	200	183	217	215	217	219
All manufactures	do.	209	192	226	224	228	229
Durable goods	do.	237	209	262	260	268	266
Nondurable goods	do.	187	179	196	195	196	198
Minerals	do.	148	130	166	160	157	163
Construction activity 1/							
Contracts, total	1935-39=100	514	422	521	533	578	577
Contracts, residential	do.	748	600	721	696	728	740
Wholesale prices 2/							
All commodities	1926=100	161	152	169	172	175	180
All commodities except farm and food	do.	153	146	162	164	167	170
Farm products	do.	170	155	178	184	187	194
Food	do.	166	155	172	175	179	182
Prices received and paid by farmers 3/							
Prices received, all products	1910-14=100	256	235	268	276	286	256
Prices paid, interest, taxes and wage rates	do.	255	248	261	263	265	272
Parity ratio	do.	100	95	103	105	108	110
Consumers' price 2/ 4/							
Total	1935-39=100	171	167	175	176	178	182
Food	do.	204	196	209	210	215	222
Nonfood	do.	153	150	155	156	158	
Income							
Nonagricultural payments 5/	Bil. dol.	205.6	195.2	212.7	213.9	221.5	
Income of industrial workers 3/	1935-39=100	367	323	405	406	415	
Factory pay rolls 2/	do.	396	350	443	442	452	
Weekly earnings of factory workers 2/							
All manufacturing	Dollars	59.27	56.29	61.99	62.38	64.15	
Durable goods	do.	63.19	59.40	66.55	66.54	68.64	
Nondurable goods	do.	54.66	52.91	56.62	57.19	58.56	
Employment							
Total civilian 6/	Millions	60.0	59.0	61.8	61.3	60.3	59.0
Nonagricultural 6/	do.	52.5	53.0	53.3	53.7	54.1	53.0
Agricultural 6/	do.	7.5	6.0	8.5	7.6	6.2	6.0
Government finance (Federal) 7/							
Income, cash operating	Mil. dol.	3,538	3,485	2,426	3,487	4,488	
Outgo, cash operating	do.	3,497	3,177	3,335	3,415	4,004	
Net cash operating income or outgo	do.	+ 40	+ 308	- 909	+ 72	+ 485	

Annual data for the years 1929-49 appear on page 19 of the March 1950 issue of The Demand and Price Situation. Sources: 1/ Federal Reserve Board, construction activity converted to 1935-39 base. 2/ U. S. Department of Labor, Bureau of Labor Statistics. 3/ U. S. Department of Agriculture, Bureau of Agricultural Economics, to convert prices received and prices paid interest, taxes and wage rates to the 1935-39 base, multiply by .93110 and .79872 respectively. 4/ Consumers' price index for moderate-income families in large cities. 5/ U. S. Department of Commerce revised figures, seasonally adjusted at annual rates. 6/ U. S. Department of Commerce, Bureau of the Census. 7/ U. S. Department of Treasury. Data for 1950 are on average monthly basis.

Commodity Highlights

Increased numbers of meat animals on farms and ranches January 1 point to a larger output of meat this year than in 1950. Prices received by farmers for milk and butterfat in the next few months are not expected to change much from present levels. The quantity of feed grains held under price support this summer will be considerably smaller than a year earlier. Redemption of wheat placed under loan is expected to continue large in the next month or two unless sales by growers are handicapped by the shortage of transportation to market. Grower prices for oranges and grapefruit are expected to average higher in March and April than in February, but prices of apples are likely to average lower because of unusually large stocks. Prices received by farmers for most vegetables for processing are likely to average higher this year than last. Prices received for new crop potatoes are expected to be moderately higher this spring than last. Export demand for the 1951 crop of flue-cured tobacco is likely to be strong.

OUTPUT AND EMPLOYMENT

Industrial production continued to expand in January in response to growing defense requirements and continued high civilian demand. The Federal Reserve Board's seasonally adjusted index of industrial production rose to 219 (1935-39=100), 1 percent above December and 20 percent above January 1950. In February total industrial output continued close to the January rate, although production in some industries was curtailed by the rail tieup early in the month. After the end of the rail strike in mid-February steel and coal output recovered to about the January levels and automobile production rose to the highest weekly rate since last October.

Durable goods production was down slightly as a result of declines in output of motor vehicles and most other metal fabricating industries. Declines in the latter reflected the initial effects of Government orders curtailing the use of critical materials for nondefense purposes. The index of durable goods output in January was 266, about 1 percent below December but 27 percent above a year earlier. Steel production continued to set new records, rising to an annual rate of 104.2 million tons of ingots and castings, compared with 100.6 million in December. Output of producers and military equipment also increased further. Shipbuilding activity and production of aircraft and railroad equipment continued to rise, and output of most building materials was maintained close to record levels. Activity in the automobile industry was down from December and well below the record high of last summer. Assemblies in January totaled about 607,000 cars and trucks, compared with 640,000 in December and the high monthly rate of 794,000 during the third quarter of 1950.

A record high plateau of output has been maintained by non-durable goods industries as a group during the past six months, the index since August having fluctuated between 194 and 198. Small changes in output of some industry groups have occurred, but these have been offset by opposite changes in the output of other groups. In January, the index rose 2 points from the previous month to 198 as output of textiles, chemicals, paper and products, and petroleum and coal products increased. Production of rubber products declined, reflecting the effects of Government restrictions on the use of rubber for civilian goods.

Production of minerals was up about 4 percent from December. Crude petroleum output rose slightly while coal production also increased.

Total expenditures on new construction in January were down seasonally, dropping to an estimated 2.1 billion dollars, 7 percent below December but 21 percent above January a year earlier. Total private outlays were down 7 percent from December but up 21 percent from January 1950. New homebuilding continued at record levels for this season of the year with outlays for such construction accounting for more than one-half of total private expenditures. Total expenditures on public construction declined 8 percent from the previous month largely as a result of declines in highway construction and in outlays on conservation and development, but these, too, were substantially above levels of a year earlier. Accelerated activity in the building of new plants for the defense effort was reflected in rising expenditures on public industrial construction and military and naval facilities. Outlays on new public industrial building were 17 percent above December and almost 4 times those of January 1950. Expenditures on military and naval facilities rose 8 percent above December and were twice those of January a year earlier.

Further restrictions on the construction of new private commercial buildings were imposed by a Federal Reserve Board order, effective February 15, requiring a 50 percent down payment on most non-residential construction. The order also required that the maturities of such loans not exceed 25 years and that they be paid off in installments over that period instead of in one payment at maturity. These credit controls supplemented earlier action taken by the National Production Authority to conserve critical construction materials which required that all new private commercial construction be subject to previous NPA authorization.

Nonfarm housing starts in January were estimated at 87,000 units. This total, while 8 percent below December, was an all time high for the month of January. The December-January decline, less than usual for that time of year, was entirely due to a drop in public housing. Private starts were up 5 percent during the period. The unseasonally high level of starts is due in part to the large backlog of builders commitments for housing that can be sold under pre-Regulation X credit terms. Anticipatory building and buying in an effort to beat the March 1 deadline prohibiting the use of certain critical materials in civilian production is also a factor. Still another factor is the uncertainty about future materials restrictions and credit terms which may be influencing many prospective new home buyers with sufficient cash to meet Regulation X requirements to buy currently instead of at some future time.

Total civilian employment in January was estimated at 59.0 million persons, 1.3 million below December but 2.1 million above January 1950. Seasonal drops in both nonagricultural and agricultural employment accounted for the decline from December. Nonagricultural employment, at 53.0 million, was 1.1 million below the previous month but 2.3 million greater than a year earlier.

The number of persons in the civilian labor force declined to
61.5 million in January, 1.0 million fewer than in December and about the
same as a year earlier. As employment dropped by more than this amount,
the number of unemployed, which is seasonally high early in the year, rose
from 2.2 million in December to 2.5 million in January. In January 1950,
about 4.5 million persons were without work.

INCOME AND RELATED FACTORS

Total personal income was up sharply in December largely as a result of an increase in dividend payments. The seasonally adjusted annual
rate of personal income, estimated at 240.7 billion dollars for the month,
was 7.8 billion dollars above November and 32.3 billion greater than in
December 1949.

Salary and wage receipts rose to an annual rate of 153.5 billion
dollars, 1.4 billion greater than in the previous month and 20.6 billion
above December a year earlier. Further expansion in manufacturing and
Government employment was largely responsible for the November to December
increase. Payments of substantial extra dividends by corporations resulted in a sharp rise in dividends and personal interest income from an
annual rate of 19.4 billion in November to 25.3 billion in December.

Dollar sales at department stores in January were up sharply from
the previous month, after allowance for the usual seasonal factors. The
Federal Reserve Board's index of department store sales, seasonally adjusted, rose to 362 (1935-39=100), equal to the all-time peak reached in
July 1950, 11 percent above December and 28 percent above January a year
earlier. The sharp rise from December, due largely to heavy purchases of
both durable and nondurable goods, was roughly comparable to the buying
wave immediately following the Korean outbreak.

Sales of all retail stores in January were estimated at 13.3 billion dollars or 9 percent above December, after adjustment for seasonal
factors and trading day differences. All major groups of stores reported
increases in sales after seasonal adjustment. Sales at durable goods
stores were up 15 percent from December with home furnishing material and
hardware stores showing advances of 22 and 17 percent respectively. Stores
in the automotive and jewelry groups registered increases of 13 percent
from the previous month. Nondurable goods stores reported a 6 percent
gain in adjusted sales. Increases for these groups were paced by apparel
stores which showed a gain of 18 percent over December. Sales at food
stores were up only slightly, while all other nondurable goods groups
showed gains ranging from 3 to 9 percent.

Consumer short term indebtedness rose 690 million dollars during December to an estimated total of 20.1 billion dollars. The increase was due largely to a seasonal expansion in charge account credit. Installment credit outstanding at the end of December, at 13.5 billion dollars, was up 174 million from the previous month. The December rise, less than half that which occurred from November to December 1949, was due largely to an expansion of credit to finance sales of appliances and other consumer durables except automobiles. Automobile sale credit, declining for the second consecutive month, was down 41 million from the end of November. Total noninstallment indebtedness of consumers increased to 6.6 billion dollars at the end of December, 516 million above a month earlier. Virtually all of the rise reflected an increase in charge account balances resulting from holiday purchases.

COMMODITY PRICES

Since mid-February, the general level of wholesale prices has been fairly stable, reflecting slight declines in farm products and foods and only small increases in wholesale prices of industrial commodities. During the week ending February 27, the BLS weekly index averaged 1.6 percent above the low preceding the effective date of the General Ceiling Price Regulation (week ended January 23, 1951). Average prices of farm products and foods at wholesale were up 2.6 percent during the five weeks ending February 27; and prices of all commodities other than farm and foods were up 1.1 percent, largely as a result of increases in prices of chemicals and fuel and lighting materials.

The rate of increase in the general wholesale price level from December to January was somewhat greater than in the previous three months as average prices of farm, food and industrial commodities registered rather substantial advances. The BLS comprehensive index of wholesale prices in January was 180.0 (1926=100), 2.7 percent above December and 18.8 percent above January 1950. Wholesale prices of farm products were up 3.5 percent from the previous month; industrial commodities, 2.2 percent; and foods, 1.8 percent.

Table 1.- Group indexes of wholesale prices, week ended February 27, 1951
with comparisons

(1926=100)

Group	Week ended Feb. 27, 1951	Week ended Jan. 23, 1951	Week ended June 27, 1950	Week ended Feb. 28, 1950	Week ended Feb. 27, 1951 percentage change from		
					Jan. 23, 1951	June 27, 1950	Feb. 28 1950
All commodities	182.9	180.0	157.4	153.0	+ 1.6	+ 16.2	+ 19.5
Farm products	201.6	196.4	165.4	159.6	+ 2.6	+ 21.9	+ 26.3
Foods	188.7	183.9	162.4	157.2	+ 2.6	+ 16.2	+ 20.0
All other than farm and food	171.1	169.3	149.2	146.0	+ 1.1	+ 14.7	+ 17.2
Textile products	181.9	180.7	137.3	138.0	+ .7	+ 32.5	+ 31.8
Fuel and lighting products	137.8	136.2	132.8	131.2	+ 1.2	+ 3.8	+ 5.0
Metals and products	188.7	188.4	171.9	168.5	+ .2	+ 9.8	+ 12.0
Building materials	227.9	225.4	203.7	193.6	+ 1.1	+ 11.9	+ 17.7
Chemicals and allied products	148.5	144.9	114.5	115.2	+ 2.5	+ 29.7	+ 28.9

Bureau of Labor Statistics.

The level of wholesale prices in late February was 16.2 percent above the pre-Korea level and 19.5 percent above a year earlier. All major groups showed increases during these periods. The largest advances were registered by textiles, chemicals, farm products and foods.

On February 13, the Office of Price Stabilization issued an amendment to the General Ceiling Price Regulation exempting from price ceilings at all levels of distribution, raw and unprocessed agricultural commodities which are currently selling at the farm at prices below the legal minima established by the Defense Production Act of 1950. Under the original price order prices of many of these commodities were exempted from ceilings only at the producer level. Major raw and unprocessed commodities affected by the amendment were corn, wheat, milk, butterfat and some types of tobacco. In processed form the commodities covered by the amendment are still subject to ceilings, although these may be adjusted upward to reflect such increases in prices paid to farmers as may occur until the legal minima are reached.

Table 2.- Group indexes of prices received by farmers,
February 15, 1951 with comparisons

(1910-14=100)

Group	Feb. 15, 1951	Jan. 15, 1951	Feb. 15, 1950	Feb. 15, 1951 percentage change from	
				Jan. 15, 1951	Feb. 15, 1950
Food grains	254	240	219	+ 6	+ 16
Feed grains and hay	222	214	171	+ 4	+ 30
Cotton	351	347	231	+ 1	+ 52
Tobacco	440	442	389	1/	+ 13
Oil-bearing crops	379	374	228	+ 1	+ 66
Fruit	204	192	186	+ 6	+ 10
Truck crops	333	324	203	+ 3	+ 64
Other vegetables	167	161	191	+ 4	- 13
All crops	283	275	215	+ 3	+ 32
Meat animals	425	391	306	+ 9	+ 39
Dairy products	285	286	250	1/	+ 14
Poultry and eggs	205	203	155	+ 1	+ 32
Wool	612	551	274	+ 11	+123
Livestock and products	340	323	257	+ 5	+ 32
Crops and livestock and products	313	300	237	+ 4	+ 32

1/ Less than one-half percent decrease.

In mid-February the average of prices received by farmers for all farm products reached a new all-time high. The BAE index of prices received on February 15 was 313 (1910-14=100), 2 percent above the previous high of 306 reached in January 1948 and 4 percent above January. Average prices received for all crops were up 3 percent from the previous month with most major groups advancing. The greatest gains were scored by food grains, fruits and feed grains. Average prices received for tobacco were down slightly from mid-January. Further increases in average prices received for meat animals, wool and poultry resulted in an average rise of 5 percent over mid-January in prices of all livestock and livestock products. Prices received for dairy products were down slightly from mid-January as a result of seasonally lower prices for milk at wholesale.

Prices received for all farm products averaged 32 percent higher in mid-February than in the same month a year ago. All major groups of commodities, except "other vegetables," showed rises from year-ago levels. Prices received for all crops were 32 percent higher, with gains for the major crop groups ranging from 10 percent for fruit to 66 percent for oilseeds. Prices received for livestock and livestock products averaged 32 percent higher than in February 1950 as prices received for wool, poultry and eggs, and meat animals advanced 123, 32 and 39 percent, respectively.

Average prices paid by farmers, including interest, taxes and wage rates were also at a new all time high in mid-February. The BAE index of prices paid, interest, taxes and wage rates was 276 (1910-14=100), 1 percent above January and 11 percent above February 1950. Higher average prices paid for food, feeder livestock, feed and building materials accounted for most of the rise from the previous month. The greater rise in prices received than in prices paid from mid-January brought the parity ratio (index of prices received divided by the index of prices paid, interest, taxes, and wage rates) to 113, three points above January and 17 points above February 1950.

Average prices paid by urban consumers' of moderate incomes reached another new high in January. The BLS revised index of consumers' prices rose 1.5 percent from December to 181.5 (1935-39=100). Average prices of all groups of goods and services advanced with foods, house-furnishings and clothing scoring the largest gains.

AGRICULTURAL EXPORTS

In 1950 the value of agricultural exports was the lowest in any post World War II year, almost 20 percent below 1949 and 27 percent lower than in 1947, the highest postwar year. In 1950 the value of food exports (including feed grains) was 1,354 million dollars or only 47 percent of the total value of agricultural exports. This compares with 3,147 million dollars or 80 percent in 1947, 2,597 million dollars or 75 percent in 1948, 2,193 million dollars or 61 percent in 1949. This downtrend in the absolute and relative value of food exports since 1947 is in contrast with an increase in the value of exports of agricultural non-foods (mostly cotton) from 810 million dollars in 1947 to 1,525 million dollars in 1950.

Compared with 1949, the physical volume of all agricultural exports declined 17 percent in 1950. There was a sharp drop in exports
of wheat (including the grain equivalent of flour) from 413 million
bushels to 251 millions. This was due to reduced takings by Western
Europe reflecting increased supplies of bread grains in these countries.
Tobacco exports were maintained at a level only slightly below 1949 but
exports of cotton increased from 5.4 million bales to almost 6 millions.

In the last quarter of 1950 the value of agricultural exports
rose 27 percent above the third quarter with all major groups showing increases. The rise resulted from an increase in quantity exported and a
smaller rise in prices.

Table 3.- Value of exports of United States agricultural
products in specified periods

Period	Cotton including linters	Tobacco, unmanu- factured	Other agri- cultural non-foods	Grain and prepa- rations	Other foods	Grand total agri- cultural
	Mil. dol.	Mil.dol.	Mil. dol.	Mil. dol.	Mil.dol.	Mil. dol.
1935-39						
Annual average	318	128	29	95	178	748
1947						
Total	427	271	112	1,881	1,266	3,957
1948						
Total	511	215	150	1,715	882	3,473
1949						
1st quarter	252	52	74	434	214	1,026
2nd quarter	272	40	84	385	225	1,006
3rd quarter	103	84	50	343	146	726
4th quarter	247	76	50	299	147	819
Total 1949	874	252	258	1,461	732	3,577
1950						
1st quarter	302	31	65	209	114	721
2nd quarter	297	44	61	181	142	725
3rd quarter	188	80	38	206	120	632
4th quarter	237	95	87	232	150	801
Total 1950	1,024	250	251	828	526	2,879

FARM INCOME

Cash Receipts for February

Farmers' cash receipts from marketings this February were about 1.9 billion dollars, 20 percent below January but 20 percent more than in February 1950. Prices of farm products averaged 4 percent higher than in January and 32 percent higher than a year ago. Sales volume was down substantially from the previous month, partly because of fewer marketing days in February.

February receipts from livestock and livestock products are estimated at 1.3 billion dollars, 10 percent less than in January but 30 percent above a year ago. Seasonally smaller marketings held cash receipts from meat animals below the January level; but higher prices accounted for a substantial percentage rise over February of last year. Dairy and poultry receipts were a little below January; but they were both well above a year ago because of higher average prices.

Crop receipts were around 0.6 billion dollars, 40 percent below January and about the same as in February 1950. Receipts from nearly all crops were down seasonally, with marketings substantially smaller and prices averaging 3 percent higher. As compared with last February, a smaller volume of crop marketings was offset by higher prices.

Cash Receipts for January-February

In the first 2 months of 1951, farmers received about 4.4 billion dollars from marketings, which was 15 percent more than they received in the corresponding period last year. Higher average prices more than offset a smaller volume of sales. Receipts from livestock and livestock products were about 30 percent above last year, with all the principal livestock commodities sharing in the increase. Crop receipts, however, totaled slightly smaller than a year ago.

1950 Summary

Realized net income of farm operators totaled 13.0 billion dollars in 1950, down 8 percent from 1949. Gross income, estimated at 32.1 billion dollars, was only slightly smaller than in 1949, but production expenses rose 6 percent to 19.1 billion dollars.

Cash receipts from farm marketings in 1950 totaled 27.9 billion dollars, or 1 percent less than the year before. Rising prices of most farm products during the second half of the year were not quite enough to offset the combined effect of lower prices earlier in 1950 and an over-all reduction of 6 percent in the volume of products sold.

LIVESTOCK AND MEAT

On February 9, a slaughter control and quota system was established by the Office of Price Stabilization. Until April 1, no one may slaughter meat animals unless he was in the slaughtering business between January 1950 and the date of the order. By March 15, all slaughterers except farm slaughterers must register with OPS. Except for farmers, after April 1 only registered slaughterers can slaughter live-stock, and their kill will be regulated in accordance with their volume of operations during the 1950 base period. Farmers who sell meat are not permitted to increase their sales. But farmers, as defined in the order, who slaughter their own livestock only for their own consumption are not subject to control.

All meats were placed under price control on January 26. Ceilings on meats are the highest prices of the period from December 19 to January 25. Sales of meat by farmers, within a specified limit of monthly sales, are not under control. Prices of live animals were not put under direct control.

In late February, market prices of most meat animals and wholesale meats receded after a steady advance that had begun two months or more earlier. Percentage increases in early February, when meat prices were first put under control, averaged somewhat greater for live animals than for wholesale products. By the end of February the percentage rise above late January was the same for live animals as for wholesale meats.

Meat production to date this year has totaled larger than a year earlier. The increase was substantial in January, but in February there was little change from last year. Hog slaughter was especially large in the first few weeks of the year, then declined sharply as the supply of old-crop hogs neared its end.

Substantially increased numbers of meat animals reported on farms and ranches January 1 strengthen prospects for a gradual increase in meat production if feed supplies and other conditions continue favorable. The 84.2 million cattle and calves were up 5 percent from the previous January and were only 1.4 million short of the all-time high in 1945. For beef cattle the increase last year was 8 percent and was mostly in beef cows and calves--for dairy cattle it was 2 percent, mostly in heifer calves. A 2 percent rise in numbers of sheep and lambs was notable because it was the first increase since an eight-year decline began in 1942. The 31.5 million sheep and lambs on hand this January were still only a little more than half their 1942 high of 56.2 million. Numbers of hogs were 7 percent larger this January than last.

Particularly meaningful to the longer outlook are the big increases in numbers of breeding stock, and especially of young breeding stock. Numbers of cows for milk did not change much but beef cows were up 10 percent. Numbers of heifers and heifer calves for milk gained 5 percent, and beef heifers 6 percent. In the stock sheep inventory, numbers of yearling and older ewes rose 1-1/2 percent, and ewe lambs, 13 percent. And numbers of sows and gilts were 4 percent larger this January.

DAIRY PRODUCTS

Prices of milk and dairy products changed little between January and February, after rising substantially from December to January. In mid-February, wholesale prices of some of the major dairy products were higher than in mid-December by the following percentages: Butter, 9 percent; cheese, 15 percent; and evaporated milk, 12 percent. The gains over a year earlier were somewhat greater, though most of the increases in prices of manufactured dairy products took place after December 1, 1950. Prices paid for milk for fluid uses in early February were contraseasonally higher than in January and were 9 percent higher than in February 1950.

Ceilings on prices of dairy products, announced on January 26, at processor and distributor levels, may move upward with advances in farm prices of dairy products until prices received by farmers for milk and butterfat reach the legal minimums at which ceilings may be established. In February, milk was 96 percent of parity and butterfat 91 percent. The actual prices received by farmers for milk and butterfat are not likely to rise in the next few months, since milk production will be showing seasonal increases. After adjustment for seasonal variation, however, prices of both milk and butterfat probably will show increases both relative to present levels and as percentages of parity. In the second half of 1951, rising consumer incomes and reduced supplies of milk products probably will generate strong upward price pressures. Ceiling levels, therefore, probably will help determine farm prices for milk and butterfat, though there are no direct ceilings on prices at the farm level.

Costs of dairy rations have increased in recent months so that even with substantial increases in milk and butterfat prices, the milk-feed price ratio was about equal to average in February and the butterfat-feed price ratio was still below average. In the last 5 months, milk production has been at an average annual rate of 119.5 billion pounds, compared with actual production in 1950 of 120.6 billions.

Since the number of milk cows in the United States is essentially unchanged from last year and the rate per cow is likely to continue near present record levels, total milk production in 1951 probably will be little different from 1950.

Consumption of fluid milk and cream is continuing larger than a year earlier. In 1951, consumption per person probably will exceed 400 pounds for the first time since 1946, compared with 393 pounds in 1949 and 340 pounds prewar. Butter consumption, on the other hand, is declining, and for 1951 probably will be only slightly over 10 pounds compared with 10.8 pounds in 1950 and the prewar level of 16.7 pounds per person. Consumption of all other dairy products is above prewar, with some at record levels.

POULTRY AND EGGS

In spite of the fact that egg production as of February 1 was about as large as last year, prices received by farmers for eggs in mid-February averaged 41.4 cents per dozen, 40 percent higher than in February 1950 and 90 percent of parity.

Several factors have contributed to this rise from a year ago. Prices of competing foods are substantially higher than last year. The population has risen by more than two million persons and Army buying has also increased.

If egg prices in the spring months exceed last year's prices by the same margins as in January and February, farmers may alter their February 1 intentions regarding the number of chickens they will raise in 1951. Their intentions were for a 4 percent decrease from last year in the number of chickens to be raised. However, recent hatchery reports even after allowing for an increase in broilers indicate a rise in production of baby chicks for farm flock replacement. This rise may reflect the improved egg-feed price ratios such as those of January and February, which usually result in increased numbers. The increased egg output following such an increase in chickens raised, if it occurs, would be available in the last 3 months of the year.

In February, poultry prices were higher than a month earlier. On the parity scale, however, the prices of chickens and turkeys are lower than any of the red meats with which they compete. In mid-February chicken prices at 26.9 cents per pound (live) were 88 percent of parity, and turkeys, at 34.5 cents per pound, were also 88 percent of parity.

On January 1, farmers intended to raise 1 percent more turkeys in 1951 than the 44.6 million they raised in 1950. Most of the increase is indicated in the North Atlantic and South Atlantic regions.

FATS, OILS, AND OILSEEDS

Prices of most leading fats and oils in February averaged higher than a month earlier. The index of wholesale prices of 26 major fats and oils (excluding butter) in February was about 250 (1935-39=100), compared with 241 in January 1951, and 217 in December, 151 in June and 146 in February 1950. It was announced February 19 that the national average support price for 1951 crop soybeans will be $2.45 per bushel, compared with $2.06 per bushel a year earlier.

The General Ceiling Price Regulation, issued January 26, 1951, was amended in February. Under present regulations, prices of unprocessed peanuts, flaxseed, butterfat and tung nuts are exempt from control as prices of these commodities are below the legal minimums prescribed in the Defense Production Act of 1950. Prices of cottonseed, which are above the legal minimum, are controlled at levels of trade beyond the producer on the basis of the highest price received by each seller in the base period (December 19, 1950-January 25, 1951). Ceilings on soybean futures on the Chicago Board of Trade and sales of cash beans, Chicago track, through a commission merchant are set at $3.33 per bushel. Ceilings at various marketing levels, including sales by farmers, are based upon the Chicago base or State levels. Base ceilings on No. 1 and No. 2 green and yellow soybeans have been set at $3.31, delivered at Chicago with differentials for the various States. Soybeans sold for seed are exempt from control. The ceiling price for soybean meal ($74 per short ton, f.o.b., cars Decatur, Illinois) is set at a level which, together with soybean oil ceilings, will reflect the legal minima for soybeans and permit equitable margins to processors.

In early February meal was selling for about $67 per ton but with the announcement of the ceiling price, sellers have advanced their prices but few sales have been made.

Specific ceilings have also been announced for crude and refined cottonseed, corn oils and crude soybean oils. The ceiling for crude cottonseed oil, f.o.b. mill, ranges from 23-1/2 cents to 23-7/8 cents depending on location. The ceiling price for crude soybean oil is 20-1/2 cents per pound, f.o.b. mill, Decatur, Illinois, plus freight to destination. The ceiling for refined soybean oil is based upon the price of the crude oil with adjustments for grade, location, and container. Ceilings for corn oil are as follows: crude, tank cars, f.o.b., Midwestern mills, 24-1/2 cents; refined, salad oil, basis f.o.b., Chicago, 27-1/2 cents. This regulation rolls back prices of these oils and in order to protect producers who normally operate on comparatively small gross margins, contracts entered into before the issuance of this order can be carried out at the contract price. The 3-cent spread between ceiling prices of crude cottonseed and soybean oils, although lower than the spread existing in the last few months, is wider than normal. It is expected that the 3-cent spread will continue to encourage the substitution of soybean for cottonseed oil necessitated by the small cottonseed and the record soybean crops.

Prices of other domestic fats, oils, and fat and oil products are controlled on the basis of their highest price for each seller in the base period. Increases in prices paid for unprocessed peanuts, flaxseed, tung nuts and butterfat (which are not controlled) up to the legal minima, may be passed on in exact dollar and cents amounts through all stages of processing. To permit imports, prices of practically all imported fats, oils (including tung oil) and their fatty acids are exempt from control so long as the oils remain in a form customarily designated by the trade as "oil."

CORN AND OTHER FEEDS

Market prices of most feeds continued upward from mid-January to mid-February, but increases generally were at a slower rate than in the last quarter of 1950. In the latter half of the month, market prices of most feed grains declined moderately. Prices of all feed grains are above the 1950 supports, but are below parity, the minimum level at which ceilings can be established on feed grains. Feed grain prices have advanced more than high-protein feeds during the past year. The market price of corn has advanced to the CCC sales price in many areas, and sales of CCC corn to domestic buyers have increased during the last 2 or 3 months.

The recently announced amendments to the General Price Regulation exempt prices of feed grains and hay in unprocessed form. Processor prices, and distributor prices of commodities in processed form are frozen at the highest level in the base period, December 19 through January 25. They may be adjusted upward to the extent that their raw material costs advance above their costs during the base period, until it is determined that the price of the raw material has reached the legal minimum. The ceiling price of soybean meal has been established at $74 per ton, bulk, in carload lots, Decatur, with differentials for quality, location and other considerations.

Stocks of the four feed grains on January 1 totaled about 102 million tons. Of this total 18 million tons were under loan or owned by CCC, about the same quantity as a year earlier. Sales of CCC-owned feed grains have been increasing in recent months and are expected to be larger during the first half of 1951 than in the same period of 1950. A substantially smaller total quantity of feed grains is going under price support this year, and it now appears likely that the quantity of feed grains held under price support this summer will be considerably smaller than a year earlier. During October-January CCC sold about 30 million bushels of corn, and on February 1 had on hand about 420 million bushels taken over from the 1948 and 1949 crops.

Heavy utilization of the big stocks of feed grains on hand January 1 is expected to leave a somewhat smaller carry-over at the close of the 1950-51 feeding year than the 31 million tons at the beginning. Most of the reduction will be in stocks of corn. Smaller stocks in Government ownership, as well as privately owned, are in prospect.

The Secretary of Agriculture announced on February 15 price supports on 1951 feed grains. The price support for corn will be 90 percent of parity at the beginning of the marketing year (October 1), with an assured minimum average support of 1.54 per bushel. The price support on corn will apply nationally, since there will be no acreage allotments in 1951. The 1951 national average price support for oats is 72 cents per bushel, barley $1.11 per bushel and grain sorghums $1.88 per hundred weight. The price supports on these grains are not subject to upward adjustment for change in parity as is the case for corn.

WHEAT

Prices received by farmers on February 15 for wheat, at $2.21, were 22 cents above the loan of $1.99 and 15 cents below the legal minimum ceiling price of $2.36. With prices substantially above the loan, large quantities of wheat under loan have been redeemed and sold on the market. This is expected to continue, and if there is sufficient transportation available only a small quantity will be delivered to CCC.

Total disappearance of domestic United States wheat in 1950-51 is expected to be about 1,015 million bushels, the smallest since 1942-43. With the supply of about 1,450 million bushels, the carry-over next July would be about 435 million bushels, slightly above the 423 million bushels July 1, 1950. The highest carry-over was 631 million bushels in 1942, and the 1932-41 average was 235 million bushels. Domestic disappearance is estimated as follows: Civilian and military food, including territorial use, about 500 million; seed, 90 million; and feed from domestic supplies, 150 million. Food use per capita may be about the same as a year earlier. Total seed requirements will be larger than last year, and feed from domestic supplies may be about the same.

Exports in the 1950-51 marketing year are now expected to total about 275 million bushels, which compares with 250 million bushels estimated earlier in the season. The export demand exceeds 275 million bushels, but the actual quantity which will be moved will be limited by the shortage of boxcars and ocean shipping, and to some extent, by the handling capacity of facilities at United States ports. Exports by June 30 of 275 million bushels would be the smallest since 1944-45 and compares with 299 million bushels in 1949-50 and the all-time record high of 503 million bushels in 1948-49.

On February 2 the Secretary of Agriculture announced a spring wheat acreage of 21.4 million acres as a guide for spring seedings. If this spring wheat acreage is seeded and if yields equal to the 1946-50 average are obtained, a crop of about 300 million bushels would be produced. This added to the 899 million bushels for winter wheat estimated in December, would total about 1,200 million bushels. The winter wheat crop has been subjected to droughty weather in the Southwest, but conditions have been mostly satisfactory elsewhere. Whether the crop in the Southwest regains growing vigor and emerges from the dormant period satisfactorily depends much upon weather conditions during the next few weeks.

Domestic disappearance of United States grown wheat in 1951-52 is expected to total about 750 million bushels. Allowing for as much as 350 million bushels for export, a total disappearance of about 1,100 million bushels would be indicated. Production in excess of this quantity would increase the carry-over July 1, 1952.

Actual estimates of areas seeded to winter wheat and rye for harvest in 1951 are available for very few other countries, but general indications denote little change in expected acreage for the Northern Hemisphere. Moisture reserves in the Prairie Provinces of Canada up to November 15 were reported at 90 percent of normal compared with 72 percent a year earlier.

FRUIT

Grower prices for oranges and grapefruit probably will average higher in March and April than in February. But prices for apples probably will decline because of unusually large stocks.

Terminal market auction prices for oranges have advanced considerably from the post-Christmas drop in early January. In late February, prices for Florida oranges were considerably below prices of a year earlier, while those for California oranges were moderately lower. With demand for oranges for processing as well as for fresh market use continuing strong, some further increase in prices, especially for Florida oranges, seems likely this winter and early spring. Total supplies of oranges remaining to be marketed after mid-February were slightly larger than at that time in 1950.

Total national supplies of grapefruit remaining to be marketed after mid-February were only slightly larger than a year earlier. Freezing weather in Texas in late January and early February severely damaged the unharvested citrus fruit of the 1950-51 crop. Most of the damage was in grapefruit limiting further utilization to processing.

Because of the reduction in the Texas crop and continuing strong demand, both grower and terminal market prices for grapefruit for fresh consumption are expected to increase during late winter and early spring.

Despite a larger-than-usual movement of apples during January, cold-storage holdings on January 31 were about 35 percent larger than the above-average holdings on January 31, 1950. Utilization of apples for processing into canned apples, applesauce, and apple juice has been large. Substantial quantities have been moved with the aid of the surplus removal and export-payment programs of the Department of Agriculture. Even with the continued help of these favorable factors, both grower and terminal market prices for the large remaining supplies of apples probably will decline over the next few months. Cold-storage holdings of pears on January 31, 1951, were about as large as the near-average stocks a year earlier, and prices over the next few months probably wil l not change much from February levels.

Stocks of frozen fruits and fruit juices in cold storage January 31, 1951 were about 53 percent larger than the stocks a year earlier and 22 per-cent larger than the 1946-50 average for January 31. Strawberries, cherries, and fruit juices comprised more than half of the stocks on January 31, 1951, and the stocks of each were much larger than a year earlier.

COMMERCIAL TRUCK CROPS

For Fresh Market

Although consumer demand continues strong, the principal reason for the unusually high prices paid for fresh vegetables this winter has been the very short supplies available. Supplies were reduced by cold weather in January and February. Indicated production of 12 of the 18 winter vegetable crops is smaller than last year, with cabbage, carrots, celery and tomatoes showing the largest tonnage decreases. Percentage decreases are sharp also for the winter crops of lima beans, beets, cucumbers, egg-plant, and green peppers. On the other hand, the winter crops of lettuce, artichokes, green peas and shallots w ere significantly larger this winter than last.

The relatively short supply of fresh vegetables may extend well in-to spring. Early reports covering acreage of the crops that account for about half of the commercial truck crop acreage for spring harvest indicate a 15 percent decrease in acreage. The largest reduction is in early spring onion acreage in south Texas, where continued dry weather largely restricted this crop to irrigated areas. Acreage of all spring crops reported to date show decreases in acreage. However, prospective acreage of several major crops such as tomatoes, lettuce and snap beans has not yet been reported.

For Processing

The Department has announced suggested guides for 1951 acreages and production of vegetables for commercial processing that take account of current stock positions and the increased civilian and military demands in prospect. Suggested acreages of 9 crops in the aggregate are 22 percent larger than the acreage planted in 1950. Special emphasis is placed on sweet corn and tomatoes for processing, with suggested acreages increased

40 percent and 35 percent, respectively, above the 1950 planted acreage.
Other acreage increases suggested are: green peas, 15 percent; snap beans,
10; and lima beans, 5 percent. No change is recommended for acreage of
beets, cabbage for kraut, cucumbers for pickles, and spinach.

It seems probable that prices paid to farmers for most, if not all,
processing crops this year will be higher than last year. For several of
the processing crops, prices received by farmers this year may well go up to
the point where they reach the legal minimums at which ceilings may be
imposed. Most of any rise in raw product cost probably will be passed on
by processors to distributors and retailers, with moderately higher retail
prices the general rule on the 1951 pack.

The Department announced on February 27 the "legal minimum" prices
for vegetables for processing, by producing areas. The prices represent the
upper limit to which processors can increase prices paid farmers and still
be able to pass the increase along in the processor's selling prices.

POTATOES AND SWEETPOTATOES

Old-crop potatoes will continue low-priced this spring, as
merchantable stocks on February 1 were still very large, despite heavy
movement in January to commercial and support outlets. Acreage of new-crop
early commercial potatoes is substantially smaller this year than last, and
new potatoes are expected to be in shorter supply. Prices received for new
potatoes, therefore, both at the farm and at retail are expected to be
moderately higher, at least through early May.

Acreage was cut sharply this year in a number of commercial areas
growing potatoes for early harvest. Unfavorable weather in Texas and
Florida, was a considerable factor in the reduction in these 2 States. Some
of the largest drops in acreage occurred in California and in North Carolina.
Farmers intentions to plant, as reported in January, indicated a reduction
of 19 percent in acreage for harvest in the late spring harvest group of
States, and 17 percent less acreage in summer-harvest areas. The January
report also showed an intended reduction of 15 percent in the planted
potato acreage in the 18 Surplus Late States and a cut of 13 percent in the
Other Late and Intermediate groups of potato States. If farmers carry out
these intentions, the surplus produced this year should be smaller than for
the 1950 crop. The 1951 crop does not have price-support, while the 1950
crop was supported in most States.

Prices received by farmers for sweetpotatoes are expected to rise
seasonally in the next few months at about the usual rate, and remain
moderately lower than a year earlier through most of the 1950 crop marketing
season. Retail prices for sweetpotatoes probably will change very little,
however.

COTTON

Trading on cotton futures markets was suspended the day following
the issuance of General Ceiling Price Regulation No. 1 on January 26, 1951
and organized spot markets did not quote prices. On January 26, the
average ten spot market price for Middling 15/16 inch was 44.49 cents--a
decrease of 0.65 cents from the record high set on January 23. The farm
price in mid-February was 41.75, (126 percent of parity), 0.44 cents higher
than in January and 1.39 cents above the mid-December price.

On March 3, OPS announced dollars and cents ceiling prices on raw cotton at all levels of distribution. The ceiling price was set at 45.76 cents per pound for Middling 15/16 inch cotton in area 1, Carolina mill points. Differentials from this price for quality and location were also announced.

Demand for the relatively small 1950 crop continues strong. Mill consumption from August 1, 1950, through February 3, 1951 totaled 5,445,299 bales. The index of spindle activity was 145.9 in January 1951, compared to 133.0 in January 1950, and reflected an average daily consumption of 42,500 and 37,400 bales, respectively. Of the 3,496,000 bales allocated for export, approximately 2,000,000 bales had not yet left this country on January 1. Total exports from August through December 31 amounted to about 1,833,000 bales as compared with 1,885,000 bales for the same period last season.

While the price of cotton used in the manufacture of 17 constructions of gray goods rose by 1.62 cents (from 42.67 cents in December to 44.29 cents in January), the average price of the cloth increased by only 1.53 cents from 92.88 cents to 94.41 cents. This represents a decrease in mill margins from 50.21 cents to 50.12 cents.

The tight supply situation has led to the establishment of a production guide of 16 million bales this year, and the Secretary of Agriculture announced 1951 planting guides of 28,400,000 acres for upland cotton and 135,000 acres for American Egyptian. Acreages in 1950 were 18,551,000 and 103,500 respectively. To provide an incentive to produce the estimated minimum desirable production of 75,000 bales of extra-long staple cotton, the Secretary announced an average price support of $1.04 a pound, through a purchase program, for Grade No. 2, 1-1/2 inches, American Egyptian cotton. In addition, the Commodity Credit Corporation is now offering to buy, for the national stockpile, extra-long staple cotton located outside the United States.

On February 14, the Secretary announced that, due to the rise in parity prices, the loan rate on the 1951 upland cotton crop is expected to average about 30 cents a pound, with a rate of 29.68 cents for Middling 7/8 inch. This rate is equal to 90 percent of January parity, and will be revised upward should parity prices advance further between January and August.

Price quotations on linters, while somewhat higher than January levels, are largely nominal. The price spread between chemical and felting grade linters narrowed in recent weeks. Despite this price movement, the supply of felting grade linters is particularly short.

WOOL

Prices for most wools at the British Dominion auctions declined slightly in early February. However, demand strengthened later in the month and by late February prices for most wools had advanced to levels near those prevailing before the decline, which were the highest ever recorded. Prices in the South American markets at mid-February were about the same or slightly higher than in late January.

Prices received by domestic growers for shorn wool averaged $1.09 per pound, grease basis, in mid-February. The average price received in February 1950 was 48.7 cents. The greater part of the 1951 clip already has been contracted for at prices considerably higher than those received for last year's clip. Contracting for 1951 wool in advance of shearing began late last summer. The annual average price received by growers for shorn wool in 1950 was 57.3 cents per pound, grease basis, compared with an average of 49.4 cents received in 1949. The 1950 average price is the second highest on record, being exceeded only by the average price received in 1918.

The Office of Price Stabilization has exempted from the General Ceiling Price Regulation sales of certain wool products when sold to defense agencies or their suppliers under contracts entered into upon the basis of invitations for bids issued on or before January 26, 1951. The items exempted are (1) raw, scoured, and pulled wool, wool top, noils, mohair, and wool waste; (2) woolen and worsted yarns and textiles; (3) articles which are made principally from woolen or worsted yarns and textiles (except those in which the woolen material is supplied by a Defense Agency).

Domestic production of shorn and pulled wool this year probably will be about 260 million pounds, grease basis, or about 113-114 million pounds, scoured basis. This would be about 13 percent less than the record production of 455 million pounds, grease basis, in 1942 but slightly more than the quantity produced last year. The expected increase in production reflects an increase of about 4 percent in stock sheep numbers during 1950. Production of wool in the United States in 1950 totaled 252.5 million pounds, grease basis, consisting of 220.1 million pounds of shorn wool and 32.4 million pounds of pulled wool.

Consumption of apparel wool by domestic woolen and worsted mills during 1950 totaled 429 million pounds, scoured basis. This was about 27 percent more than the quantity consumed the previous year but was about 30 percent below the record consumption of 610 million pounds in 1946. Consumption of carpet wool, all of which is imported, also was considerably higher than during 1949. Consumption of such wool, 196 million pounds, scoured basis, was 21 percent greater than during 1949 and only 6 percent below the record consumption of 208 million pounds in 1948.

The United States imported considerably more wool in 1950 than during 1949. Imports for consumption of dutiable (apparel) wool totaled 250 million pounds, clean basis, or 402 million pounds, actual weight during 1950. This compared with 155 million pounds, clean basis, or 262 million pounds, actual weight, imported during 1949. The quantity of apparel wool imported was equivalent to over 70 percent of domestic consumption. Imports for consumption of duty-free (carpet) wool amounted to 217 million pounds, clean basis, or 315 million pounds, actual weight. This was almost double the quantity imported during 1949.

TOBACCO

Burley tobacco auctions for the 1950 crop were near closing by late February and prices for the season averaged 48.8 cents per pound-- 8 percent above the 1949 season average and fractionally above the prewar record for the 1948 crop. Dark air-cured tobacco (types 35-36) auctions were interrupted by cold weather conditions in early February. Prices for these types through late February averaged 23.2 cents per pound compared with 27.8 cents a year earlier. The larger proportion of lower quality tobacco resulting from unfavorable weather in the Kentucky-Tennessee area during the growing season lowered the general price average for the dark air-cured types 35-36 and the fire-cured types 22-23. Fire-cured tobacco in the Eastern District (type 22) and Western District (type 23) averaged 30.9 and 26.5 cents per pound, respectively, for quantities auctioned through late February. Average prices for both types were a little above those for approximately the same quantities of marketings in the 1949 season and individual grade prices were generally higher. The 1950 crop of Virginia fire-cured (type 21) was all sold by March 1 and auction prices averaged 36.3 cents per pound for the season compared with 33.5 cents last season. Cigar binder tobacco prices in the Connecticut Valley averaged lower than last season's while Pennsylvania filler prices for roughly one-third of the crop sold by mid-February probably averaged near or slightly above a year earlier.

On February 27, the 1951 acreage allotments for flue-cured and Burley were increased above those announced in late November 1950. If yields per acre are approximately the same as in the recent 5-year period, the 1951 crops of these types, together with the carry-overs, will provide increased supplies to meet the strong domestic and export demand. The 1951 allotments for flue-cured at 1,120,000 acres and for Burley at 470,000 acres are approximately 14 and 12 percent larger than last year's. The parities and price support for the 1951 crops will exceed those applying to the 1950 crops, mostly because of the rise in the index of prices paid by farmers, interest, taxes, and wage rates during the last few months.

The exports of unmanufactured tobacco from the United States in 1950 totaled 476 million pounds valued at 250 million dollars. Exports volume was 2 1/2 percent less than in 1949, but total value was down by less than 1 percent. The export demand for the 1951 crop of flue-cured is expected to be strong. Flue-cured accounted for four-fifths of total tobacco exports in 1950.

In January tax-paid withdrawals of cigarettes, as indicated by stamp sales, were nearly 16 percent above the record January total last year. Also cigars, snuff, and smoking and chewing tobacco combined were indicated as being above last January. During the last quarter of 1950 tax free removals of cigarettes for overseas forces and United States possessions rose sharply over the last quarter of 1949. The President's tax program recommended an increase in the Federal excises on cigarettes and cigars. The present rate of $3.50 per 1,000 (7 cents per package of 20) would go to $5.00 per thousand (10 cents per pack) if the recommendation should be adopted. The tax rates on cigars vary according to intended retail prices.

U. S. Department of Agriculture
Washington 25, D. C.

OFFICIAL BUSINESS

BAE-DPS-3/51-5600
PERMIT NO. 1001